PROOF

INAUGURAL POEM SUITE

CORNELIUS EADY

T P

TUPELO PRESS

NORTH ADAMS, MASSACHUSETTS

Proof: Inaugural Poem Suite

ISBN: 978-1-961209-79-4 (HC)
978-1-961209-80-0 (Paper)
Cover and text design by Allison O'Keefe
Front cover: Photo by Sarah Micklem
First paperback edition: July 2026

Tupelo Press
P.O. Box 1767
North Adams, Massachusetts 01247
(413) 664-9611 / Fax: (413) 664-9711
editor@tupelopress.org / www.tupelopress.org

Contents

Foreword

Herein roils the reckoning of Cornelius Eady's *Proof*. Herein thrives a poetic proclamation of public intent. First orated by the poet on the bracing New Year's Day of 2026 to celebrate new Mayor Zohran Mamdani's inauguration, *Proof* commemorates a New Yorker's dire quest for just governance. Each stanza wields a stubborn joy against the inertia of *"not now"* politics. His verses furnish evidence that true progress seeks articulation in imaginative expression on the way to finding realization in deed. Indeed, it is a call to *imagine...*

Imagine the multilingual, many gendered, multihued multitudes of New York gathering themselves together in the midst of a darkening storm. *Imagine* them in hundreds of voting booths, penciling their vote in thousands of tiny printed bubbles to answer the call of change. *Imagine* their call answered eagerly with new representation. Now, imagine a blues-throated troubadour—one raptured in the throes of Black sermon's "call and response" ready to regale them with their much deserved "Amen!" Here, visible for all to read, roars that anthem for the army of voters that chose ballot boxes to reclaim their boroughs.

The cipher of poems in this chapbook is a chorale of civic and personal witness. From 19th-century African Methodist Episcopalian congregations to the tense moment a dread-headed professor is stopped and interrogated beneath a heritage of Tubman starlight.

From Robert Frost's and Elizabeth Alexander's presidentially poetic inaugural moments to Aretha Franklin's regal crown that witnessed the day "ain't no way" found a way. From *Raisin in the Sun*'s knife in sheep's clothing to the surreptitiously bigoted bone of *The Tingler* that threatened enthralled audiences. From overturned expectations of judicial oversight to the tense triggers of the Second Amendment and the 911 call's rigged racial expectations.

Cornelius was surprised when he received the email from the Mamdani campaign, inviting him to give poetic testimony at his inauguration. He'd cast a vote for the candidate, but like any savvy New Yorker, he thought this too-good-to-be-true request smelled like a possible scam. It wasn't until he verified the offer that he was convinced it was real. Even then, dear reader, he almost decided to demur and pass the opportunity on to another poet—something he has done with many other literary opportunities. But, fortunately for us, he decided to bring his own insight to this singular, historic task of literary citizenship and brandished his pen in support.

Eady has been stepping up in the name of community and citizenship for decades. He served as co-founder, along with Toi Derricotte, of Cave Canem Foundation, fostering the development of hundreds of Black poets for 30 years. He's stepped forward as a board member and director of New York's legendary Poets House, leading it through challenging transitions. His years of teaching elevated him to Chair of Excellence at University of Tennessee, and he now serves as a Chancellor on the American Academy of Poets. His playwriting, poetry, performance, and literary stewardship have inspired generations of writers and institution builders.

As said, Cornelius was surprised by the offer to write an inaugural poem for a charismatic, optimistic New York mayor. But those who have been paying attention were not. He has, for a lifetime, woven word and deed into Gotham's identity with an acute sense of history and an ear tilted toward the sound of hard-won, plain-talked witness. Herein writhes a grit-graced testimonial to resilience.

Dear reader, in one line of this volume, Eady wonders about *what work it is to stand alone*. But herein, he has taken us all to stand with him until each of us *looks at this version of America in the eyes*. And so, the poems offered here stand with us face to face—and dare us to live into the best of our imagination.

Tyehimba Jess

Proof

Inaugural Poem Suite

Proof

You have to imagine it:

Who said you were too dark/too
Large? Too queer/too loud?

Who said you were too poor/
Too strange? Too fat?

You have to imagine it:

Who said you must keep quiet?
Who heard your story, then
Rolled their eyes?

Who tried to change your name
To invisible?

You've got to imagine:

Who heard your name
And refused to pronounce it?
Who checked their watch
And said "not now"?

James Baldwin wrote:

"The place in which I'll fit
Will not exist
Until I make it."

New York, city of invention,
Roiling town, refresher
And re-newer,

New York, city of the real,
Where the canyons
Whisper in a hundred
Tongues,

New York,
Where your lucky self
Waits for your
Arrival,

Where there is always soil
For your root.

This is our time.

The taste of us/the spice of us
The hollers and the rhythms and
The beats of us.

In the echo of our
Ancestors,
Who made certain we know
Who we are.

City of Insistence,
City of Resistance,

You have to imagine:

An army that wins without
Firing a bullet,

A joy that wears down
The rock of *no*.

Up from insults,
Up from blocked doors,
Up from trick bags,
Up from fear/up from shame,
Up from the way it was done before.
You have to imagine:

That space they said wasn't yours.
That time they said you'd never own.
The invisible city lit, on its way.
This moment is our proof.

Written for the Inauguration of Zohran Mamdani,
January 1st 2026, NYC

The Inaugural Poem, January, 1961

Robert Frost is lit by sun; a brighter grey
In the black-and-white weather, his hair
Wild poet's grass.

Poetry doesn't matter here; ask the
Temperature, ask the capitol dome,
Ask the dark suits surrounding
His odd bird body, waiting to hear
America, American.

Now he squints, and his shiver tells us
What work it is to stand alone.
And then there is a moment nobody knows–

It could be the sound of a stroke
Making a blender of his throat.
It might be the brat foot of tumble
Kicking away the stool
In his inner ear.

If tough luck blows his page away.
If his heart rattles its last full measure.
If these words he's now pulling from
Memory dam up.

He is the man holding up the music,
The parade, the champagne.
He is making everyone hold
Their breath and think of
How gravity taunts the acrobat.

PRAISE FOR THE INAUGURAL POET, JANUARY, 2009

Perhaps it's an impossible task
On an impossible day. A young poet
Fixes her gaze along the plaza,

Looks at this latest version of America in the eyes,
Looks in the camera at all the places we've touched
Or torched.

Sees who's come to this roll call:
The out of the wood-works, the I never dreamts,
The I never thought we'd live this longs,

Stands in the sharp report of weak January sun.
The poet probably knows
This family is hers.

The poet probably knows
Before she cuts history to forty-four lines,
Before the capitol has more proof
Of what bullets and ropes couldn't stop,

She has to straighten her back. She needs to take
A deep breath. A Black woman is here.
All the Black women in her are here to sing.

For Elizabeth Alexander

Aretha Franklin's Inauguration Hat

Look at that hat, my mother might have said,
Sitting in that bunker the living room had become,
Her favorite shows interrupted by the sight

Of this woman, who once sang my sister through
One of her major heartbreaks—an I give then
Take-away man

With a truth which rose through the house—I was too young
To know which kind of truth, really, and my sister
Was now learning the words-her belly would swell from it—

Ain't no way, aint no way, sang the girl who was slightly
Older than my sister, old enough to teach it.
Ain't no way, ain't no way

The needle scratched, and scratched again.
It's not too far-fetched to think of it breaking skin,
A rush of something toxic, tear-raising.

Remember when she didn't want to tell us
But told us by playing that damn record all day
Over and over in her bedroom, that's the woman under

That hat I'd tell my mother, if she'd asked.
That church hat.
That testimony hat.
That Black woman's hat.

September 20, 1830: Black leaders convene in Philadelphia at Rev. Richard Allen's AME Church for the first gathering of what would come to be known as the "Colored Conventions" movement, a series of formal meetings of Black Americans dedicated to advancing racial justice. The first convention was called in response to exclusionary laws passed in Ohio the year before. Over the next six decades, more than two hundred state and national conventions were held.

We As People

In Ohio,
Black folk can walk free,

But you still have
The rights
Of a mule,
A chicken,
A blood hound—

Ever see a blood hound
Cast a vote?
Ever see a piglet
Try to write some law?

We as people
Have to stop waiting,
While the mobs sweep
The Cincinnati streets
Of Black skins, Black thought,
Black laughter, Black prayers,
Black homes, Black children,

Black song, packing your bags
With bruises, skinning your
Breath with knuckles, the tar
Dipped, lit and torch tossed

On the front porch of your
Consideration. Some of us
Took that hint and flew,

Exit, exile, Exodus.
Others wonder why Jesus
Let the cops chase their fancy
Unpunished,

But We as people have to stop asking
A flood to stop being a flood,
Expecting a hurricane to grow
Some manners.

We've come to Philly to find out
What happens
When we stop running,
And we start talking
Among ourselves.
What better selves
Do we knit?

When you open the doors
To a shelter,
After a bad storm has passed,

Ain't that air sweet? Even if the
Town is in splinters? Ain't
You happy that storm tried its level best
But couldn't stop your heart?

Overturned

What did you hear
That got you talking raw?
You got that low cloud look,
Got that heart-nicked stare.

Like the flora got voted
From under your feet.
Like someone told you a story,

Maybe the wrong story.
Palm trees where there should
Be pine. And now you doubt

Everything. Don't you hate
Doubting everything? There's
An unease the body radiates

When it can't put a finger
On a lie. You got that pickle
Wince, my friend,

You look like
You lost the directions
To where you from.

Self-Portrait as the Professor of Astronomy, Miscegenation and Critical Theory at the New Negro Escapist Social and Athletic Club Center For Graduate Studies by Rashid Johnson

Well, said the officer, as he hands my ID back.
My dreads are clean, but are they too long?
My suit, a professor's armor, does he consider it stolen?
He won't say: let's see you talk your way out of this.
He won't say: I bet your lady is white.
He won't say *boy*, but we both know his knuckles itch
To spell it. It is night, and we are under the stars.
I know the one Tubman used to steer herself clear of
Perhaps this man's Great Grandfather. I profess
To my students that she never lost a single soul,
She would arrive like moonlight, and ghost away
The field hands. You aren't from around here, he says,
But what I hear is, there's nobody around.
I know we are parked under the drinking gourd,
And suddenly, I'm not new.

Lucia Whalen's Teachable Moment

The woman whose 911 call brought the police to Prof. Henry Lewis Gates' House. It was later revealed she never used race in her description of the men she saw.

That old bad dream—
You open your mouth,
and out comes what you know

you can never take back.

I never said boo. But turn on
any television, buddy,
click the damn mouse.

Who said what? My breath
never bounced ugly up,
a piss-off solar flare
off the satellite, into that despatchers' ear.

Never, never.

But now the neighbors ask: Who
brung The Way-Back gal?
The Antebellum dunce?

The Racist Bone

I know this to be a real thing, because
When I was a kid, my big sister took me
To the Capital Theater, in my home town
Of Rochester, NY,

And there was a movie that afternoon,
The Tingler, which starred Vincent Price,
And what I remember best about the film
Was that it was about this extra, insect-like gland, that

We all appeared to have been born with,
But nobody but sci-fi movie scientists knew about.
If it wasn't fed properly, it would crawl up
Your leg, and choke you to death with its claws!

Your only hope was, if you saw it coming, and knew
What it was, you could scream—loud.
Which we did, when it crawled across the screen.
Then the lights blacked out, and Vincent Price

Shouted it had skittered off the screen, hungry—
  which it hadn't;
The Capital was the Black movie house—25 cents a seat,
The last drop of profit squeezed from the theatrical run.
No need to pull Mr. Castle's hokey string and rubber model

Down the aisle for the likes of us.
In our heads *The Tingler* scurried, our darkest screams,
The horror we know, but won't talk about,
From the mouth of the corpse

Like a weevil, looking for a home.
So many characters perished
In that movie—they never believed they had it in them
Until those pinchers closed.

The Second Amendment

Driving out to Long Island over the Williamsburg Bridge
I spot the young white men on the rooftop.
There's a bottle neck as the ribbon of feeder lanes
Merge, and the boys on the roof laugh, one of them
Cradles a mock rifle, another cocks his thumb and forefinger
Into a pistol—the way of cowboys and Indians, the way of kids,
Wishes whistling, aimed and fired—the driver with the hijab,
The driver with the dreads, the driver with the darkest skin?
Burst water balloon, hacked limb, fucked-up puppet, cut free.

The boys are not quite ready. This is not the day after the dress
Rehearsal, the day someone regrets putting on a bright hat,
Or zigs instead of zags, or wisely detours the parade
Or street fair, then wishes they could drive the afternoon back
To its tame beginnings and choose again. This is the day we will
Ride, spotless, though their blank mercy.

What Do You Call

You know, the white guy
In the film version of *Raisin in the Sun*,
Pudgy balding head
Who comes to tell
The Black family
Not to move to the
White Chicago suburb.
The man who smiles
With the knife,
Who IS a knife,
But fools them for
A second, because
They're looking at him
The way he expects
Them to look at him.
Later, as they mop
Up the blood, they replay
What he said: that he
Was elected by his neighbors,
Because he's the guy that
Can get his foot in the door,
Whipped and rumpled,
Like he's been apologizing
Since he popped out of his
Mother's womb, like he's a
Close, personal friend of sorry.

He's sorry now, in his wilted suit.
This is the way the knife

Gets through the door, and
He sits there, as they
Think, maybe this ain't a
Knife in sheep clothes, baaa
Baaa, baaa; such a foolish-looking,
Goofy little white guy.
A small part of them, quietly
Embarrassed they're even
Thinking that about him.
They can barely hold their
Manners in check, and that's
His trick, the trick of the knife
You don't see until you're cut.
And the strangest thing
About this, the damn thing
Is how meek he still looks
After he cuts, and cuts again.
Dun as a female robin,
His tongue slices and whittles.
He is singing the song of his
Tribe, money if you stay,
Fire if you come, and they think;
How did a white robe, a tinder cross,
And a lit gas can trot through
Their door? A pack of Dobermans
Couldn't have done a neater job,
Except that Dobermans of course, never
Apologize.

About the Author

Cornelius Eady is the author of numerous books of poetry, including *Hardheaded Weather* (G. P. Putnam's Sons, 2008), a nominee for an NAACP Image Award; *Brutal Imagination* (G. P. Putnam's Sons, 2001), a finalist for the 2001 National Book Award in Poetry; *The Gathering of My Name* (Carnegie Mellon University Press, 1991); and *Victims of the Latest Dance Craze* (Ommation Press, 1986), selected for the Academy of American Poets' 1985 Lamont Poetry Prize by Philip Booth, Louise Glück, and Charles Simic. He has received the Academy of American Poets' Wallace Stevens Award (2025), which recognizes lifetime achievement in poetry; a Lifetime Achievement Award from Furious Flower in 2024; and numerous other honors and recognitions, including an NEA Fellowship in Literature; a John Simon Guggenheim Fellowship in Poetry; a Rockefeller Foundation Fellowship to Bellagio, Italy; and the Prairie Schooner Strousse Award.

In 1999, Eady's *Running Man*, a music-theatre piece co-written with jazz musician Diedre Murray, was a finalist for the Pulitzer Prize in Drama and awarded a 1999 Obie for best musical score and lead actor in a musical. A production of *Brutal Imagination* (with a score by Diedre Murray) won the 2002 Oppenheimer Award for the best first play by an American playwright. As a songwriter, Eady's pandemic folk song project *Don't Get Dead*, recorded with his Trio, was released in 2021 by June Appal Recording. His work and songs have been featured on NPR, BBC Radio 4, and the PBS Newshour.

With fellow poet Toi Derricotte, in 1996, Eady co-founded Cave Canem Foundation, a nonprofit organization committed to cultivating the artistic and professional growth of Black poets; fostering community across the diaspora; and facilitating a nurturing space in which to learn, experiment, create, and present. The National Book Foundation awarded Cave Canem the 2016 Literarian Award for Outstanding Service to the American Literary Community, and in 2026, the organization received a $350,000 humanities grant from the MacArthur Foundation.

Before recently retiring from academia, Eady taught at several prestigious universities and colleges, most recently serving as Chair of Excellence in the English Department at the University of Tennessee, Knoxville. Previous appointments include, among others, the Miller Family Endowed Chair in Literature and Writing and professor of English and theatre at the University of Missouri–Columbia and director of the Poetry Center at the State University of New York at Stony Brook. Currently, he is a Chancellor of the Academy of American Poets and Vice President of the board of directors of Poets House, where he served as Interim Director in 2021–22.

Acknowledgments

These poems first appeared, sometimes in slightly different versions, in the following publications. My thanks to these publishers and editors:

"The Inaugural Poem, January, 1961" first appeared in *Valparaiso Poetry Review*.

"Praise for The Inaugural Poet, January, 2009" first appeared in the *Brooklyn Rail*.

"Aretha Franklin's Inauguration Hat" first appeared in *Think: Poems for Aretha Franklin's Inauguration Day*, ed. Patricia Spears Jones (*Bomb* magazine).

"We as People" first appeared in *The 1619 Project*, created by Nikole Hannah-Jones (One World).

"Overturned" was selected for *The Best American Poetry* series, ed. Terrance Hayes (Simon & Schuster).

"Self-Portrait as the Professor of Astronomy, Miscegenation and Critical Theory at the New Negro Escapist Social and Athletic Club Center For Graduate Studies by Rashid Johnson" first appeared in *Ursula* magazine.

"The Racist Bone" and "What Do You Call" first appeared in *Poetry*.

"The Second Amendment" first appeared in the *Southampton Review*.